CURIOUS CREATURES

The words and all the pictures in
this book are original and have been
specially commissioned for Tesco.

Published by
Tesco Stores Limited
Created by Brilliant Books Ltd
84-86 Regent Street
London W1B 5RR
www.brilliantbooks.co.uk

First published 2001

Text and illustrations © 2001 Brilliant Books Ltd

Printed by Printer Trento S.r.l., Italy
Reproduction by Colourpath, England

ISBN 1-84221-148-X

1 3 5 7 9 10 8 6 4 2

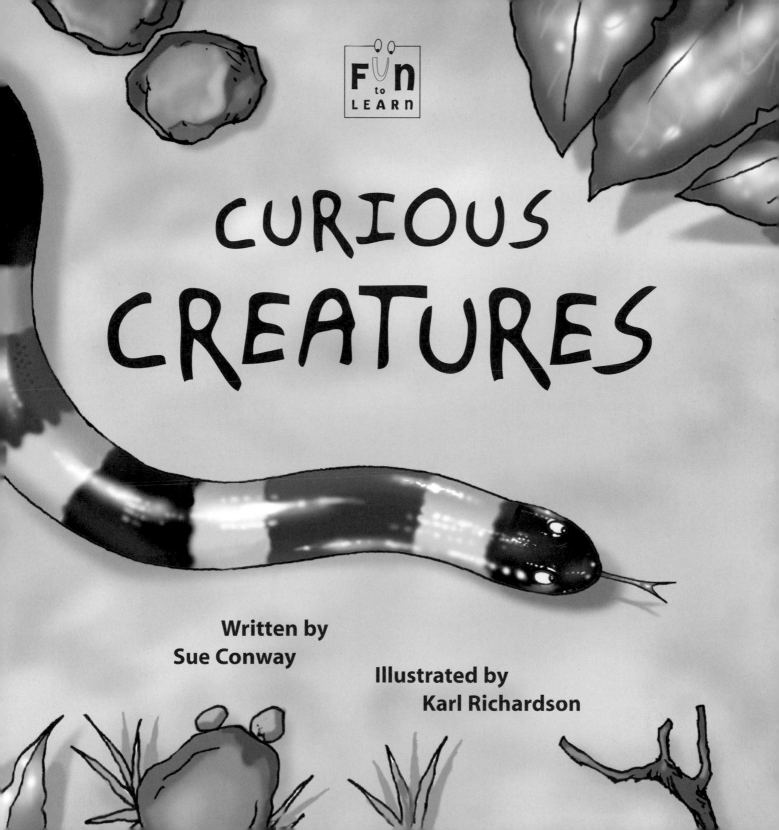

CURIOUS CREATURES

Written by
Sue Conway

Illustrated by
Karl Richardson

Chameleons

There are 89 different kinds of chameleon.
Many of them live on a tropical African
island called Madagascar.

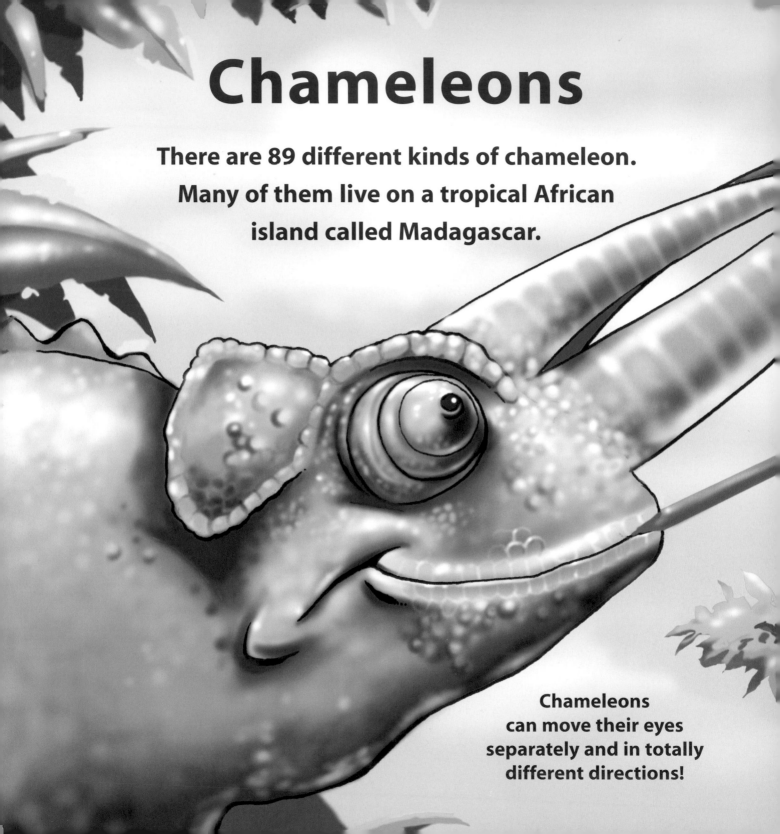

Chameleons
can move their eyes
separately and in totally
different directions!

A chameleon's tongue is longer than its body and can whizz out to catch a poor little bug in a hundredth of a second.

Chameleons can change the colour of their skin to blend in with their surroundings. Now you see me...!

Bats

Bats are very good at flying – but they're
not birds, they're furry mammals!

Bats are not totally blind, but
they work out where they are by
squeaking, and then listening
to how the echoes bounce
off objects around them.

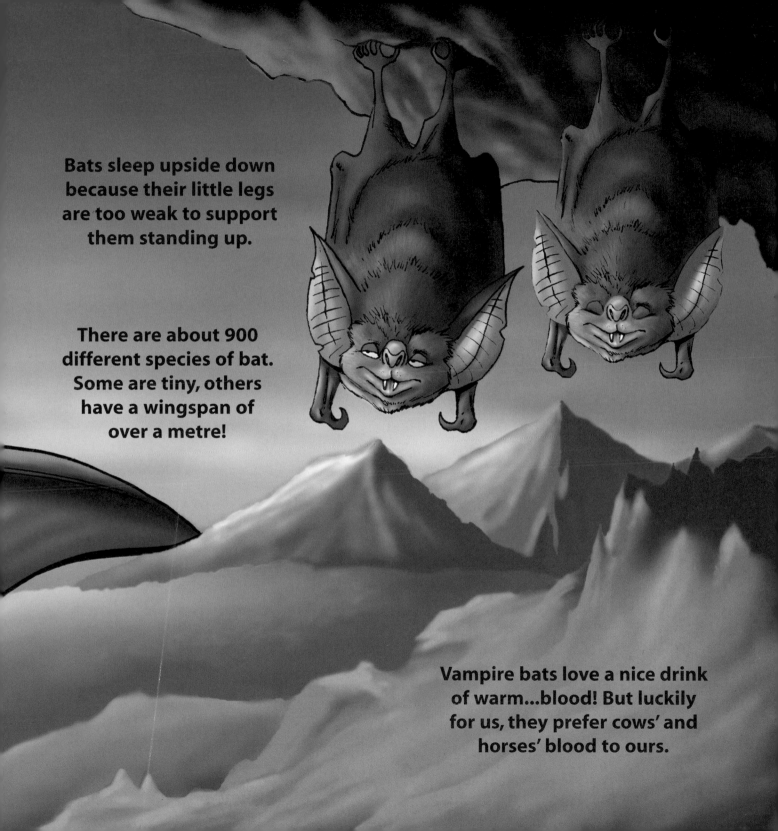

Bats sleep upside down because their little legs are too weak to support them standing up.

There are about 900 different species of bat. Some are tiny, others have a wingspan of over a metre!

Vampire bats love a nice drink of warm...blood! But luckily for us, they prefer cows' and horses' blood to ours.

Frogs

Frogs lay their eggs – called frogspawn – in ponds. Tadpoles hatch from the eggs and eventually turn into frogs, which can hop about quite happily on land.

A South American kokoi frog contains enough poison to kill thousands of people!

Local hunters puts its poison on their arrows to make them extra deadly.

Boy frogs make a right racket in order to attract girl frogs. The green frog can be heard from nearly 1km (²/₃ mile) away!

Using their strong back legs, frogs can leap up to ten times their own body length.

Whales

Blue whales are even bigger than the largest ever dinosaurs, but they are mammals – just like us.

A blue whale can hear a friend
calling it from as far away as 1,600km
(1,000 miles) – that's the distance
between Britain and Africa!

Whales don't have teeth.
They filter all their food
through a sort of giant bony
sieve called a baleen plate.

They live on
krill which are
a bit like tiny
prawns. In one
day they eat
enough to make
about 50,000
prawn cocktails!

A baby blue whale drinks
about two bathfuls of it's
mother's milk every day!

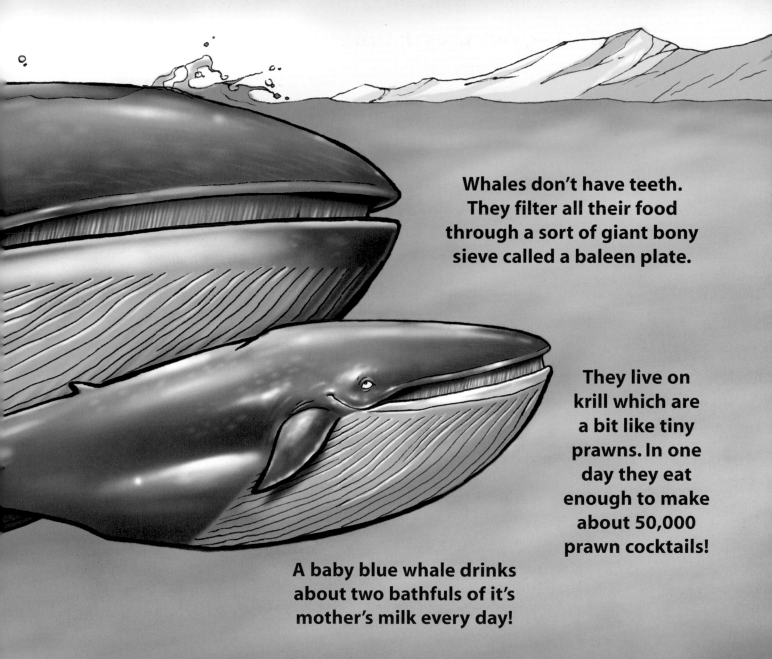

Snakes

All snakes are predators. They poison or squeeze their victims to death... and then swallow them whole!

A giant python once swallowed a whole donkey. It didn't need to eat again for months!

The tree-living paradise snake from Asia uses the element of surprise to catch its prey. It hurls itself from a high branch and glides through the air.

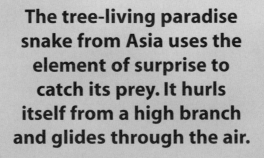

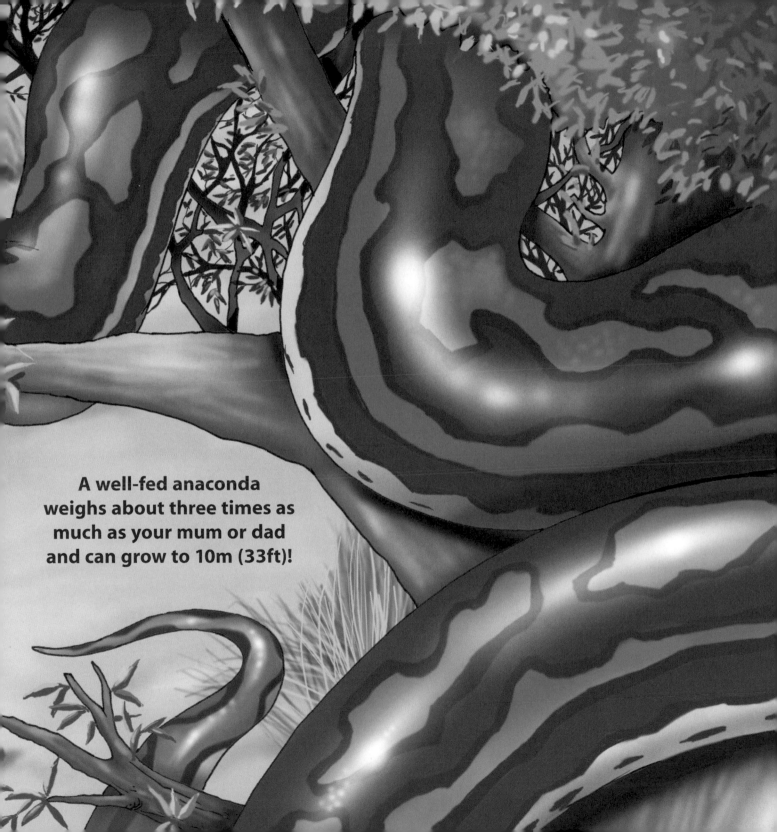

A well-fed anaconda weighs about three times as much as your mum or dad and can grow to 10m (33ft)!

Dolphins

Dolphins live in groups and chat away to each other using a great variety of squeals, buzzes, clicks and grunts.

The killer whale is actually a dolphin! It eats penguins, seals and fish and can swim faster than most ships!

Every dolphin has its own voice – a whistling sound that other dolphins are able to recognise.

Dolphins don't need to drink. They can get all the water they need from the fish and squid they eat.

Like bats, dolphins use sound to find their food and work out where they are.

Crocodiles

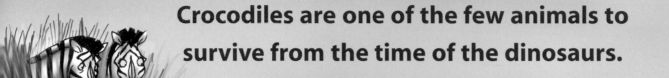

Crocodiles are one of the few animals to survive from the time of the dinosaurs.

As a crocodile's teeth wear down they are replaced by new ones. In a lifetime, a croc can get through 50 different sets of gnashers!

Crocodiles love lying in the sun. If they get too hot, they just open their mouths and they soon cool down.

A fully grown Nile crocodile can eat a whole zebra for its lunch!

Crocodiles aren't any good at chewing, so they drag their prey into the water and drown it. Then they tear off chunks of flesh and swallow them whole.

Sharks

Sharks are feared the world over. But in fact, it's quite rare for them to eat people!

A shark's skin is very rough. If you stroke it the wrong way it's like sandpaper and it might even cut your hand and make it bleed!

The largest shark is the whale shark. It can grow to be as long as a very, very big lorry.

The great white shark has incredibly strong jaws, and razor-sharp teeth that are as long as your fingers.

Sharks have an amazing sense of smell. They can sniff out one drop of blood in the sea from 100m (330ft) away.

Birds of Prey

Birds of prey feed on other animals, but luckily for us, they usually go for fairly small creatures.

Vultures are really greedy. Sometimes they eat so much that they become too heavy to fly.

Peregrine falcons are the speediest animals in the world. They can swoop down on their prey at more than 300km/h (200mph)!

An Andean condor is the heaviest bird of prey. A big one probably weighs as much as you and has a wingspan as wide as most bedrooms.

A hawk can spot a mouse while soaring as high as 300m (1,000ft) above it.

Spiders

Spiders range from teensy-weensy creatures to humungous hairy horrors!

All spiders are poisonous, but only about 30 species can bite humans. And luckily for us, only a few – like the funnel-web spider – are actually deadly!

Spider's silk is so strong, it can hold more weight than steel thread of the same thickness.

The goliath bird-eating spider of South America is as big as a dinner plate! It likes to snack on lizards, mice and even birds.

Some spiders have oily feet to stop them getting stuck to their own webs.

Guess what!

1 What animal can grow to be 55m (180ft) long? (As long as four lorries!)

Clue: It wriggles.

2 Which bird has a beak longer than its body?

Clue: Hmm-hmm-hmm.

3 How many puppies were in the biggest litter in which they all survived?

Clue: It's not as many as 101!

4 Which fish are so vicious that they will attack any animal, however large?

Clue: They're not very big, but they have razor-sharp teeth.

5 What animal has as many as 750 legs?

Clue: It's a creepy-crawwwwwwwwly,

6 What animal had a wingspan of 12m (39ft)?

Clue: Luckily, it's extinct!

7 What animal can jump 130 times its own height? (That's like your mother or father jumping over 40 double-decker buses piled on top of each other!)

Clue: Feeling itchy?

8 What animal never seems to sleep?

Clue: It lives under water and is very clever.

9 Which land animal is the noisiest?

Clue: If you were naughty, you might be called one!

10 What animals breed at the fastest rate?

Clue: They are tiny and green, and real pests.

Answers: 1 A bootlace worm. **2** A sword-billed humming-bird. **3** A foxhound had 23! **4** Piranhas – fortunately, they don't live in Britain! **5** A millipede. **6** A pterosaur – they were like giant flying lizards and were much bigger than pterodactyls. **7** A flea. **8** A type of porpoise, called Dall's porpoise. **9** A type of monkey – not surprisingly, it's called a howler monkey! **10** In one year a single aphid could, in theory, produce 822 million tons of descendants – three times the weight of every person in the world put together! Luckily, a lot of them die!